THE Perils OF PASSIVITY

FRANK HAMMOND

The Perils of Passivity

by Frank Hammond

ISBN 10: 0-89228-160-X
ISBN 13: 978-089228-160-2

Copyright © 2004. Revised 2012.
Impact Christian Books

IMPACT CHRISTIAN BOOKS, INC.
332 Leffingwell Ave., Suite 101
Kirkwood, MO 63122

WWW.IMPACTCHRISTIANBOOKS.COM

Unless otherwise indicated, all scripture quotations are taken from the Amplified® Bible (AMPC). Copyright © 1954, 1958, 1962, 1964, 1965, 1987 by The Lockman Foundation. Used by permission. www.Lockman.org.

Scripture quotations identified KJV are from the KING JAMES VERSION of the Bible.

ALL RIGHTS RESERVED

The Perils of Passivity

How does an evil spirit gain entrance into one's life? It is essential in warfare to understand the weapons and tactics of one's enemy. The same is true for spiritual warfare. We are exhorted to put on the complete spiritual armor and stand against the "wiles" of the devil. His wiles are his *methods* or *plans* to assault us. We must work...

> "To keep Satan from getting an advantage over us; for we are not ignorant of his wiles and intentions."
>
> 2 Cor. 2:11

In scripture we are warned against giving the devil any advantage:

> "Leave no [such] room or foothold for the devil [give no opportunity to him]."
>
> Eph. 4:27

In order to be successful in deliverance ministry, it is essential that we discover the ways in which evil spirits gain entrance into a person's life. It is obvious that a demon cannot enter and indwell an individual at will; otherwise each of us would be hopelessly demonized. There must be some sort of opening. Demons are limited by spiritual law, so there has to be a legal right for demons to gain entrance.

It is important for the one receiving deliverance to gain insight into how demons gained their entrance; otherwise, he will not know how to close doors against the demons' attempts to return.

Common "gates" through which demons enter are:

Family Gate — *Things that were wrong and lacking.*

Sin Gate

Trauma Gate

Undisciplined-Life Gate

Religious Gate

Relationship Gates

Occult Gate

Although there are other gates, I am convinced that the main gate through which demons gain entrance is "passivity." Not only is this a gate through which demons enter, but passivity enables indwelling demons "squatters rights;" (those allowed to settle without right or title or payment of rent); their presence in God's temple goes unchallenged! And we are His temples!

Passivity is the lack of vigilance.

> "… **be vigilant and cautious at all times, for that enemy of yours, the devil, roams around like a lion roaring [in fierce hunger], seeking someone to seize upon and devour."**
>
> 1 Pet. 5:8

In other words, we must maintain a *plan of aggression* against the devil. It is a big mistake to think that if we leave the devil alone he will leave us alone.

Synonyms and phrases for passivity are: not active; lacking in energy or will; complacency; indifference; laziness; don't care, don't feel up to resistance; unresponsive, nonparticipating; apathetic, unassertive, stoic, bound (unable or unwilling to respond).

One of the biggest challenges that confronts a deliverance minister is passivity in the person to whom he is ministering. It is very difficult to minister deliverance to a passive person. The person's will *must be activated* or failure is certain. Active faith is essential in receiving anything from God: "So be subject to God. Resist the devil [stand firm against him], and he will flee from you" (JAMES 4:7).

ACTIVE FAITH

Jesus required faith in those who came to Him for deliverance. Initially, He refused the request of the Syrophonecian woman for deliverance for her little daughter who was "miserably and distressingly and cruelly possessed by a demon!" (MATT. 15:22). But when the mother demonstrated faith, Jesus said to her,

> "O woman, great is your faith! Be it done for you as you wish. And her daughter was cured from that moment."
> Matt. 15:28

Then, there was the father who sought deliverance for his son who had seizures. Jesus said, "[You say to Me], If You can do anything? [Why,] all things can be (are possible) to him who believes!" (MK. 9:23). So, it is important for the one seeking deliverance to have active faith, demonstrated by a strong declaration of belief in God's promised deliverance, a strong confession of faith that God will deliver him, and a *warrior stance* against the devil and all indwelling spirits.

Aggressive Love for God

Throughout scripture we find that God expects us to be aggressive. First of all, we are to be aggressive in our love for Him.

> "And you shall love the Lord your God with all your [mind and] heart, and with your entire being, and with all your might."
>
> Deut. 6:5

Love is not passive; not mere feelings or words, but deeds. "Little children, let us not love [merely] in theory or in speech but in deed and in truth (in practice and in sincerity)" (1 JOHN 3:18). In loving God our desire must be towards Him, our delight in Him, and our dependence upon Him. It must be our constant joy to think of Him, to read His Word, to talk to Him in prayer, and to serve Him. Our love must be active, even aggressive.

Aggressiveness Against...
the World and the Flesh

Our enemy is threefold — the world, the flesh and the devil. We must take a definite stand against each. In fact, there is a close connection between the three. When we yield to fleshly lusts or cater to the cadence of the world, we give place to the devil. We cannot afford to let our guard down and become passive towards any of these foes. We must say with Paul,

> "But far be it from me to glory [in anything or anyone] except in the cross of our Lord Jesus Christ (the Messiah) through Whom the world has been crucified to me, and I to the world!"
>
> Gal. 6:14

> "And those who belong to Christ Jesus (the Messiah) have crucified the flesh (the godless human nature) with its passions and appetites and desires."
>
> Gal. 5:24

> "So kill (deaden, deprive of power) the evil desire lurking in your members [those animal impulses and all that is earthly in you that is employed in sin]…"
>
> Col. 3:5

AGGRESSIVENESS AGAINST… THE DEVIL AND DEMONS

Some Christians seem to think, "If I leave the devil alone then he will not notice me, and he will leave me alone." Wrong! The devil has a horrible plan for each of our lives. If we ignore him, he will be left to carry out his wiles against us without challenge or resistance. When one becomes a believer in Christ, he *automatically* becomes a Christian soldier.

When a soldier joins the army he goes immediately to the quartermaster who outfits him with the proper uniform and battle gear. Notice the following high-lighted active verbs that pertain to the Christian warrior and his warfare. There is no place for passivity in spiritual warfare!

As Christian soldiers we are issued spiritual armor:

> "Put on God's whole armor [the armor of a heavy-armed soldier which God supplies], that you may be able successfully to stand up against [all] the strategies and the deceits of the devil."
>
> Eph. 6:11

We are ordered to *wrestle* against invisible opponents in the supernatural sphere (Eph. 6:12) and "to stand your ground on the evil day [of danger]" and " to stand [firmly in your place]" (Eph. 6:13).

Furthermore, we are given orders to "Resist the devil [stand firm against him], and he will flee from you." (James 4:7). The Greek word for "resist" is from the Greek word *anthistemi* from which the pharmaceutical drugs called antihistamines derive their name. An antihistamine *stands against* or *resists* histamine which causes allergies. We are to have an automatic, built-in resistance to the schemes of the devil!

Scriptures teach us to *resist the devil* in steadfast faith:

> "Withstand him; be firm in faith [against his onset—rooted, established, strong, immovable, and determined]..."
>
> 1 Pet. 5:9

We are furthermore charged to be aggressive in the employment of our spiritual weapons,

> "For the weapons of our warfare are not physical [weapons of flesh and blood], but they are mighty before God for the overthrow and destruction of strongholds..."
>
> 2 Cor. 10:4

The words of Jesus addressed to all believers are especially pertinent and powerful: "And these attesting signs will accompany those who believe: in My name ***they will drive out demons...***" (Mark 16:17, emphasis mine). Every aspect of our spiritual walk is to be characterized by *aggressive action*. If anyone were ever justified in resting on his laurels it was the Apostle Paul; however, he did not become complacent over past achievements or derailed by past failures. His vow was:

" I press on to lay hold of (grasp) and make my own, that for which Christ Jesus (the Messiah) has laid hold of me and made me His own. I do not consider, brethren, that I have captured and made it my own [yet]; but one thing I do [it is my one aspiration]: forgetting what lies behind and straining forward to what lies ahead, I press on toward the goal to win the [supreme and heavenly] prize to which God in Christ Jesus is calling us upward."

Phil. 3:12–14

Why Are Some Passive?

How can passivity be reversed? How is the will strengthened? Why is it important to be aggressive? These questions deserve an answer. Let us examine several ways by which passivity is fostered.

➢ Love

Love is essential to a stable personality. Passivity is found in individuals who have not been loved adequately. A child must be conceived in love, birthed in love and brought up in a love environment. Otherwise, such an individual is destined to become schizophrenic;[1] a divided personality, sometimes introverted and sometimes extraverted; sometimes passive and sometimes aggressive.

The passive personality is withdrawn, filled with self-pity and imprisoned in "self." When this individual swings into an opposite personality, his aggressiveness is negative, expressing itself in rebellion, resentment, bitterness, hatred and anger.

---

1 It was the Hammond's contention (and revelation, as explained in *Pigs in the Parlor* and other teachings), that most people are in need of deliverance from a pattern of spirits called "schizophrenia," in some form or fashion; that this pattern is Satan's ***master plan*** for the human race. In their experience in ministering for four decades, they determined that most individuals battle a network of demonic spirits which include both the passive and the aggressive, due to the spiritual roots of rejection and rebellion from early in life. See their book *Pigs in the Parlor*, their DVD video *The Schizophrenia Revelation*, and their Audio CDs *Breaking Demonic Strongholds* and *The Deliverance Series*. **www.impactchristianbooks.com/frank**

➢ Discipline

A disciplined life is not passive, so discipline in the formative days of one's life is essential to strengthening the personality. Some children require more discipline than others, so discipline must be done in keeping with the individual's need. A child cannot learn self-discipline on his own. He must be disciplined so that he will become self-disciplined. That is why the scripture says,

> "a child left undisciplined brings his mother to shame."
>
> Prov. 29:15

Without proper discipline a child will become unruly and his behavior will embarrass his parent. Likewise, the Heavenly Father disciplines His children,

> "For the Lord corrects and disciplines everyone whom He loves, and He punishes, even scourges, every son whom He accepts and welcomes to His heart and cherishes. ... For the time being no discipline brings joy, but seems grievous and painful; but afterwards it yields peaceable fruit of righteousness to those who have been trained by it..."
>
> Heb. 12:6, 11

The discipline of a child is not simply a means of punishment for wrong-doing but a way of instruction. "To discipline" means "to teach." A disciple is a learner. Therefore, proper discipline must be consistent and administered in love. The father and mother themselves must be disciplined in order to correctly administer discipline to their child.

Our book, *Kingdom Living for the Family*, has a section that deals with the proper discipline of children. Scriptures and examples advocating spanking are given.

Worldly wisdom is more and more equating spanking as abuse. Although some children are physically abused through unreasonable beating, God's wisdom teaches that corporal punishment is the desirable form of discipline.

When our book on family relationships was being published overseas, we received a letter from those in Europe who were translating the book. We were advised that a law had been passed there that made it illegal for children to be spanked, so they needed our permission to omit examples given of children being spanked. It was agreed that the examples could be omitted as long as the scriptures advocating spanking were retained. The following Proverbs show God's approval for spanking children and His council to do so:

> **Withhold not discipline from the child, for if you strike and punish him with the [reedlike] rod, he will not die. You shall whip him with the rod and deliver his life from Sheol.**
> Prov. 23:13–14

> **The rod and reproof give wisdom, but a child left undisciplined brings his mother to shame.**
> Prov. 29:15

> **Discipline your son while there is hope, but do not [indulge your angry resentments by undue chastisements and] set yourself to his ruin.**
> Prov. 19:18

> **Train up a child in the way he should go [and in keeping with his individual gift or bent], and when he is old he will not depart from it.**
> Prov. 22:6

> **Foolishness is bound up in the heart of a child, but the rod of discipline will drive it far from him.**
> Prov. 22:15

Self-discipline includes the mind, emotions, volition, physical body, stewardship of money and material possessions, and one's relationship with God.

Anyone who has not received adequate or proper discipline as a child, and recognizes that he is lacking in self-discipline, should make it a priority to exercise self-discipline. With some it may be necessary to submit to an appropriate authority for supervision and correction until self-discipline is achieved.

▸ Boundaries

Each of us need to set and observe spiritual, physical and moral boundaries. God's commandments are spiritual boundaries. There are passive people who claim, "I can't keep from committing adultery... I can't keep from smoking... I can't keep from drinking." God's Word makes no allowances for the weak-willed. Every commandment addresses the will. Everyone is responsible to obey God's commandments — no excuses accepted! Our bodies are temples indwelled by the Holy Spirit. We must not defile our bodies but rather keep them under discipline. Over indulgence with food, excessive use of alcohol, use of tobacco products and failure to exercise are sins against our bodies and are invitations to demons. Those who have not accepted and observed God's protective boundaries are vulnerable to the perils of passivity.

▸ Death To Self

Jesus said,

> "Whoever does not persevere and carry his own cross and come after (follow) Me cannot be My disciple... So then, any of you who does not forsake (renounce, surrender claim to, give up, say good-bye to) all that he has cannot be My disciple." Luke 14:27, 33

Paul said,

> "And those who belong to Christ Jesus (the Messiah) have crucified the flesh (the godless human nature) with its passions and appetites and desires."
>
> Gal. 5:24

Again,

> "That each one of you should know how to possess (control, manage) his own body in consecration (purity, separated from things profane) and honor. Not [to be used] in the passion of lust like the heathen, who are ignorant of the true God and have no knowledge of His will..."
>
> 1 Thess. 4:4–5

No wonder Satan's goal is to lure us into bondages to "self." Every demon is a self-oriented spirit. For example, pride is *self-exaltation*; lust is *self-indulgence*; rebellion is *self-rule*; resentment is *self-vindication* and inferiority is *self-pity*. Every demon named can be given a synonymous name beginning with a "self" prefix.

There can be two opposite and possible bondages to self. First, exalting yourself above others.

> "...in the true spirit of humility (lowliness of mind) let each regard the others as better than and superior to himself [thinking more highly of one another than you do of yourselves]."
>
> Phil 2:3

Second, thinking yourself inferior to others through failure to recognize your uniqueness as a member of Christ's body:

> "If the foot should say, Because I am not the hand, I do not belong to the body, would it be therefore not [a part] of the body?"
>
> 1 Cor. 12:15

We must not be passive when it comes to the crucifixion of self. Paul expressed it for us:

> "I have been crucified with Christ [in Him I have shared His crucifixion]; it is no longer I who live, but Christ (the Messiah) lives in me…"
>
> Gal. 2:20

Death to self is a choice of our wills that we must make daily. Passivity will keep a person from giving himself totally to Christ.

➤ Responsibility

If one is to conquer passivity, he must learn to bear responsibility. Children develop a life-long pattern of behavior when they are taught to bear responsibilities within the home. It is important training when a child is required to carry out the trash and keep his room straight. Some parents are over protective. They make all the decisions for their children, and fail to train them in bearing responsibilities.

Children untrained in bearing responsibility develop an expectation that others are responsible for them. As adults they continue to look to others to do everything for them. They whine, "Pray for me. Cast out my demons." When confronted with the need to take some initiative and responsibility for themselves, they are prone to go from place to place seeking someone who will cater to their every need. This is blatant passivity, "For every man shall bear his own burden" (GAL. 6:5, KJV).

▸ Goals

Our lives have a purpose in God that is far greater than our personal ambitions and pursuits,

> "So that we who first hoped in Christ [who first put our confidence in Him have been destined and appointed to] live for the praise of His glory!"
>
> Eph. 1:12

Only by recognizing and discovering God's eternal plan for our lives will we be able to set life-goals worthy of our calling. We must be neither ignorant of — nor passive towards — God's purpose for our being here.

> "So we are Christ's ambassadors, God making His appeal as it were through us."
>
> 2 Cor. 5:20

King David expressed his goal for his life:

> "One thing have I asked of the Lord, that will I seek, inquire for, and [insistently] require: that I may dwell in the house of the Lord [in His presence] all the days of my life, to behold and gaze upon the beauty [the sweet attractiveness and the delightful loveliness] of the Lord and to meditate, consider, and inquire in His temple."
>
> Ps. 27:4

The Apostle Paul stated his goal:

> "[For my determined purpose is] that I may know Him [that I may progressively become more deeply and intimately acquainted with Him, perceiving and recognizing and understanding the wonders of His Person more strongly

and more clearly], and that I may in that same way come to know the power outflowing from His resurrection [which it exerts over believers], and that I may so share His sufferings as to be continually transformed [in spirit into His likeness even] to His death…"

Phil. 3:10

Paul also voiced a determined goal for his ministry in Corinth:

"For I resolved to know nothing (to be acquainted with nothing, to make a display of the knowledge of nothing, and to be conscious of nothing) among you, except Jesus Christ (the Messiah) and Him crucified."

1 Cor. 2:2

➤ Work Ethic

Without a strong work ethic a person drifts into passivity. He becomes the classic couch potato. He has a welfare mentality. He is like the man described in Prov. 26:14,

As the door turns upon its hinges, so does the lazy man [move not from his place] upon his bed.

In more extreme cases, he expects his needs to be handed to him on a consistent basis.

As we have seen in other safeguards against passivity, a strong work ethic is best developed in adolescence. We have all witnessed the mistake made by parents who do not teach or require their children to work. Such children develop no initiative, and either learn in later life in "the school of hard knocks" the importance of work or else remain lazy and passive, expecting others to feed, clothe and put a roof over their heads.

There were lazy members in the Ephesian church who had even resorted to stealing, and to them it was said,

> "Let the thief steal no more, but rather let him be industrious, making an honest living with his own hands, so that he may be able to give to those in need."
>
> Eph. 4:28

The time has come for us to quit making excuses for not being productive. Purpose to be productive each day that the Lord grants you life. Let us pray with the Psalmist...

> "So teach us to number our days that we may get us a heart of wisdom."
>
> Ps. 90:12

➤ Doer of the Word

Judging by the Word of God, there are many deceived members in the church today.

> "But be doers of the Word [obey the message], and not merely listeners to it, betraying yourselves [into deception by reasoning contrary to the Truth]. For if anyone only listens to the Word without obeying it and being a doer of it, he is like a man who looks carefully at his [own] natural face in a mirror; For he thoughtfully observes himself, and then goes off and promptly forgets what he was like."
>
> Jas. 1:22–24

All sorts of excuses are made for not being doers of the Word. We've known those who say, "It may work for others, but it does not work for me." Or, "I am a victim of my past. I was brought up in a dysfunctional family... my father was an alcoholic", or, "Don't except anything of me... this is just the way I am."

Either we are doers of the Word or we are sitting on our hands being passive about what God expects of us.

➢ Comparison with Others

Scripture is referring to the unwise decision of one member of the body to compare himself with others when it says,

> "If the ear should say, Because I am not the eye, I do not belong to the body, would it be therefore not [a part] of the body? ... But as it is, God has placed and arranged the limbs and organs in the body, each [particular one] of them, just as He wished and saw fit and with the best adaptation."
>
> 1 Cor. 12:16, 18

Through comparison to others a valid member of the body of Christ is rendered passive. He sits down on the inside because he does not have the talent, personality or where-with-all to do what he sees another doing. He forgets that he is *unique*, for God made him so. It is important for us to realize that we are not expected by God to do what other members do, but to only do what God has called and equipped us to do.

A church's ministry is greatly limited because of the widespread practice of comparison. Many do little more than warm a pew because they deem themselves ill-equipped and unqualified to do anything more. Because one cannot carry a tune or stand up to teach or to preach, does not mean he has no responsible function in the Body of Christ.

> "But instead, there is [absolute] necessity for the parts of the body that are considered the more weak... God has so adjusted (mingled, harmonized, and subtly proportioned the parts of) the whole body, giving the greater honor

and richer endowment to the inferior parts which lack [apparent importance], So that there should be no division or discord or lack of adaptation [of the parts of the body to each other], but the members all alike should have a mutual interest in and care for one another."

1 Cor. 12:22, 24–25

"...when they measure themselves with themselves and compare themselves with one another, they are without understanding and behave unwisely."

2 Cor. 10:12

➤ Spoken Curses

"Death and life are in the power of the tongue" (Prov. 18:21). So, there are such things as spoken curses: curses which others have spoken against us, curses which we have spoken when we have said evil things about others and curses that we have spoken against ourselves.

If, as a child, you were cursed and abused by evil words you may have come to believe those words and decided "I am no good. I am a failure. I never do anything right. It were better if I had not been born," etc. Then, you acted on those words of curse and withdrew into self-pity, inferiority, insecurity and passivity.[2]

To overcome spoken curses one should seek God's forgiveness for having said negative things about others; forgive those who have spoken curses against you, and begin to confess what God says about you. Say, "By the grace of God I am accepted in Christ. I have been foreordained to adoption as God's dear child, and I am redeemed through His blood unto eternal life. I renounce Satan and break every curse spoken by me and against me."

2 See *The Father's Blessing* by Frank Hammond. Impact Christian Books, Inc.
   www.impactchristianbooks.com/frank

➤ The Grace of God

A common companion to passivity is unworthiness. There are still too many recipients of God's grace who feel that they must do something to merit God's favor. Grace is commonly defined as "unmerited favor." It is all that God did for us through Christ that we were unable to do for ourselves.

I vividly remember how I resisted when God called me into the ministry. I didn't feel worthy to be a preacher. I boarded a train and traveled over a thousand miles in my effort to escape God's presence. When I finally gave up, my first sermon was about Jonah who tried to run away from God's call. I tried to bargain with God, "Let me be a businessman and make lots of money. I will give generously to the support of Your Kingdom." But God didn't want what I could produce; He wanted me. It was not a matter of what I could do for God but what He could do for me.

None of us are worthy within ourselves. That is what the Cross is all about.

> "For it is by free grace (God's unmerited favor) that you are saved (delivered from judgment and made partakers of Christ's salvation) through [your] faith. And this [salvation] is not of yourselves [of your own doing, it came not through your own striving], but it is the gift of God..."
>
> Eph. 2:8

If we are to conquer unworthiness with its accompanying passivity we must embrace the grace of God. We must confess that He took the initiative in our salvation, and we cannot do anything to gain or retain that salvation. The opening verses of Ephesians bear the good news that we are chosen, predestined, adopted and accepted in the Beloved, to the praise of the glory of His grace.

➢ Analyzing

To analyze is to divide into separate parts for the purpose of examination so that a judgment can be made. When, for example, the one who presents himself for deliverance is told that a particular demon has been discerned, he turns the discernment this way and that way in his mind, eventually rejecting the discernment. He then sits passively, unwilling to put forth any effort to get the demon out.

The deliverance minister is responsible for spiritual diagnosis and prescribed treatment. Unless the candidate accepts the diagnosis and follows the prescribed treatment, the minister's hands are tied. Even though the deliverance minister may sometimes err in discernment, still the demon challenged will not come out if he is not there! It is best to go along with whatever discernment is given. It is better to challenge a demon that may not be there, than to leave unchallenged one that IS there.

The analyzer is prone to gravitate from one deliverance minister to another, seeking to hear what he wants to hear and rejecting everything that disagrees with his own diagnosis. Analyzing everything, and receiving only what self agrees with, holds one in deception and renders oneself passive. The willingness to *cooperate* is vital to successful deliverance.

➢ Time Is Running Out

> "For even though by this time you ought to be teaching others, you actually need someone to teach you over again the very first principles of God's Word. You have come to need milk, not solid food."
>
> Heb. 5:12

The old adage is true: "He who learns and learns but never knows is like him who plows and plows but never sows." Either we are growing in spiritual maturity or we are back-sliding or, at best, standing still. Standing still is the result of passivity. The hymn "Higher Ground" expresses the zeal needed: "I'm pressing on the upward way. New heights I'm gaining every day. Still praying as I onward bound. I'm pressing on to higher ground."

> "And from the days of John the Baptist until the present time, the kingdom of heaven has endured violent assault, and violent men seize it by force [as a precious prize—a share in the heavenly kingdom is sought with most ardent zeal and intense exertion]."
>
> Matt. 11:12

➢ "I Can't" vs. "I Won't"

There are those who, when challenged to make an effort, say, "I can't." How can anyone ever say, "I can't" when God's Word clearly says,

> "I have strength for all things in Christ Who empowers me [I am ready for anything and equal to anything through Him Who infuses inner strength into me…"
>
> Phil. 4:13

The one who seeks to excuse himself with "I can't" is really saying "I won't." Again, we affirm the necessity of the involvement of a *person's will* in spiritual battle. Others can help us in our battles, but we must ourselves engage the enemy if we expect to gain and maintain the victory. Spiritual warfare excludes passivity.

➢ Not Teachable

The first requirement for a good deliverance is a teachable spirit. There are times when the person seeking deliverance needs correction, and if such a person refuses correction it is fruitless to continue. For example, an experienced deliverance minister knows that homosexuality is demonic, for he has dealt with such demons. But there are homosexuals who will not agree that their perverse lifestyle is sinful and has opened them to demons. How then can these be delivered?

There are some who equate correction with rejection. One day a couple of Jehovah's Witnesses came to my house. I explained how I had ministered deliverance to other Jehovah's Witnesses, and that if they would repent I would minister deliverance to them. They were offended saying "You don't love us, or you wouldn't talk to us like that." I replied, "I DO love you, and I want you to be set free. Jesus said, 'The truth will set you free'" (JOHN 8:32). But to them correction was perceived as rejection, and they remained in their bondage.

Again, there are those who want deliverance from some demons but not from others. Such a one might say, "I want deliverance from insomnia, but leave my caffeine demon alone." When a person is in agreement with ANY demon, he is not teachable and rendered incapable of receiving a thorough deliverance.

There are others who want to tell the deliverance minister what the problem is and how to (or how not to) go about it. Unless he can have it his way he will withdraw into passivity, refusing to cooperate.

> "Obey your spiritual leaders and submit to them [continually recognizing their authority over you], for they are constantly keeping watch over your souls and guarding your spiritual welfare, as men who will have to render an account [of

their trust]. [Do your part to] let them do this with gladness and not with sighing and groaning, for that would not be profitable to you [either]."

Heb. 13:17

▸ Complacency

We never get to the point of spiritual maturity when there is no need to grow further. As Paul expressed it, his goal was to know...

"...Christ Jesus my Lord and of progressively becoming more deeply and intimately acquainted with Him [of perceiving and recognizing and understanding Him more fully and clearly]."

Phil. 3:8

Our spiritual development is progressive as long as we live in these temporal bodies.

Scripture uses the analogy of the athlete, the runner and the boxer, to illustrate how we must maintain our zeal.

"Do you not know that in a race all the runners compete, but [only] one receives the prize? So run [your race] that you may lay hold [of the prize] and make it yours. Now every athlete who goes into training conducts himself temperately and restricts himself in all things... Therefore I do not run uncertainly (without definite aim). I do not box like one beating the air and striking without an adversary. But [like a boxer] I buffet my body [handle it roughly, discipline it by hardships] and subdue it..."

1 Cor. 9:24–27

If we ever become complacent over the level of maturity we have attained, then we become passive and quit the race. We become satisfied with less than the best and quit growing spiritually. Thus, we play right into the hands of the devil.

When we traveled in ministry to developing countries we experienced many miracles of deliverance and healing, a much greater anointing than we ever experienced here in the States. When we testified of the mighty miracles of God we were asked, "Why don't you do that here?" It was the same problem that Jesus faced in His home town. There was little faith. "And He did not do many works of power there, because of their unbelief (their lack of faith in the divine mission of Jesus)" (MATT. 13:58). Most of us still need an increase of faith. It is no time for complacency and passivity.

➢ Faith, Hope And Love

1 CORINTHIANS 13:13 speaks of *faith*, *hope* and *love*. These are three cardinal virtues of Christian life that must be guarded and maintained at all times. Whenever we see ourselves begin to slip in anyone of these virtues it should be a warning sign to find out what has happened and to correct it.

Faith is our spiritual foundation. It is the basis of our relationship with God. Hope is an "anchor of the soul" (HEB. 6:19). Without hope, a joyful and confident expectation of our future in Christ, we are like ships without anchors, destined to be at the mercy of life's storms and headed for shipwreck. Love is *the* cardinal virtue. Jesus summarized the ten commandments into love for God and neighbor.

> And He replied to him, You shall love the Lord your God with all your heart and with all your soul and with all your mind (intellect). This is the great (most important, principal) and first commandment. And a second is like it: You shall love your neighbor as [you do] yourself.
>
> Matthew 22:37–39

Conclusion

Some have made deliverance their ultimate goal in life. Deliverance is not a final goal, it is only a sub-goal on the way to fulfill God's purpose in life. Deliverance is no more the goal for us than for the children of Israel escaping their bondage in Egypt. God said to Pharaoh, "Let my people go, that they may serve Me..." (Exod. 7:16). There was a purpose for Israel beyond their escape from bondage, and there is a purpose in God for each of us.

God has called us to war, and we must be vigilant, for we are not ignorant of Satan's devices. If we lack a definite plan of aggression, we have become passive to some degree.

Remember, God called King David to war, and although he won many battles and defeated thousands of enemies, there was a time when he became passive. "In the spring, when kings go forth to battle... David remained in Jerusalem" (2 Sam. 11:1). It was in this time of passivity that temptation overtook him. David saw Bathsheba bathing, lusted after her and committed adultery with her, having her husband murdered in an attempt to cover up his sin. Psalm Fifty-One tells us of his pain from a defiled conscience and the repentance that restored his relationship with God.

As we have shown, passivity will block deliverance. The ways in which passivity works have been observed over our years in deliverance ministry. This list is not by any means complete, but it will give the reader some idea of how to look for yet other roads leading to passivity.

One of the biggest challenges confronting a deliverance minister is the passive person. It is *essential* for a person's will to be involved; therefore, we always have the individual make a confession of his faith and his stand against Satan's kingdom. For some, this is all that is needed to activate his will. If a confession and prayer are not enough, we urge the passive candidate to breathe or cough out the spirits as we identify them. A spirit is breath, and expelling the breath is appropriate and often effective. Even then, with a few extremely passive persons, this is not enough to get them into an active role. It has been found helpful to put hand pressure on appropriate parts of the body, e.g. top of the head, shoulders, abdomen, back, arms or hands. Of course, it should go without saying, that the touching of a person be done with utmost discretion.

Please pray the following prayer with me to defeat passivity in your life…

Prayer and Confession

Heavenly Father, I am Your child through faith in the Lord Jesus Christ. I believe, Lord Jesus, that you are the Son of God. You are the Savior come in the flesh to destroy the works of the devil. You died on the cross for my sins and rose up from the dead. I now confess all my sins, known and unknown, and repent of each one. I especially confess the sin of passivity, and I call upon You to give me strength to overcome every aspect of passivity in my life. I ask You to forgive me and cleanse me in Your blood. I do believe that Your blood cleanses me now from all sin. Thank You for redeeming me, cleansing me, and sanctifying me in Your blood.

I purpose in Christ to be aggressive in my love for God, in the crucifixion of my flesh, in my death to self, and in my resistance of the devil and his demon powers. You, Lord Jesus, have given me life, and I now give my life to You. My heart's desire is to glorify Your name. In Your strength I will love, obey and serve You all the days of my life.

Satan has no place in me or power over me. I, therefore, command every spirit of passivity and every related spirit to leave me now, in the name of Jesus.

Amen!

The Passive Family of Demons

Passivity

Weak-willed
Stoic
Introverted
Apathetic
Unresponsive
Bondage
Timid
Shy
Withdrawn
Escape

Not Disciplined

Spoiled Brat
Ill-mannered
Pampered
Coddled
Immature or "Baby"
Neglected

Deprived of Love

Rejection
Fear of rejection
Self-rejection
Self-accusing
Fear of God's rejection - (Ultimate Rejection)
False personalities
Lust (sexual & material)
Rebellion
Selfishness
Root of bitterness
Resentment
Anger
Hatred
Unforgiveness
Retaliation
Murder
Paranoia
Distrust of others
Suspicion
Fear of exposure
Fear of losing control
Fear of demon manifestations
Fear of the unknown

The Passive Family of Demons

No Boundaries

Loose
Lying
Dishonest
Immoral
Undisciplined
Laziness
Addictions:
    Tobacco
    Alcohol
    Drugs
    Caffeine
    Sugar

Criminal
Evil
Wicked
Rebellion
Lawless
Sexual obsessions
Spend-thrift
Stingy
Greedy
Lust
Body idolatry
Anorexia
Unresponsive

No Death to Self

Self-awareness
Selfishness
Self-gratification
Self-indulgence
Pride
Unteachable
Self-deception

No Responsibility

Dependence on others
Indolent
Idle
Non-aggressive
No ambition
Procrastination
Shiftless
Childish
Weak-willed

The Passive Family of Demons

Without Goals

Aimless
Irresolute
Vacillating
Wanderer
Purposeless
Undedicated
Worldly

Non-Doer of Word

Forgetting what heard
Spiritual deafness
Self-deception
Self-diagnostician
Self-satisfied
Short-sighted
Complacency

No Work Ethic

Unorganized
Empty
"I can't..." (change, resist the devil, submit to God)
Lazy
Without goals
Day dreamer
Fantasy
Procrastination
Prisoner of the past
Worthless

Comparison

Inadequate
Inept
Inferior
Hatred of self
Misfit
Superiority
Pride
Ego
Vanity

Complacency

Self-satisfied
Smug
Self-deceived

The Passive Family of Demons

Curses

Spoken Curses
Undeserving
Not Good Enough

Without Grace

Guilt
Works Salvation
Fear of Lost Salvation
Fear of Judgment

Analyzation

Rationalize
Nitpicker
Distrust of Others
Anti-Submissive
Unteachable
Disagreeable
Confrontation

Not Teachable

Closed personality
Pride
Self-deception
Know-it-all

Time Running Out

Procrastination
Lazy
Put-it-off
Evasion
Immature
Infantile
Fear of responsibility

I Can't vs. I Won't

Quit
Give up
Weak-willed
Unbelief
Rebellion
Self-will
Stubborn
Hopeless
Deferred hope
Despair
Depression
Despondent
Discouragement
Death wish

FRANK HAMMOND BOOKS & EBOOKS

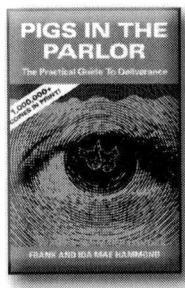

Pigs in the Parlor   0892280271

A handbook for deliverance from demons and spiritual oppression, patterned after the ministry of Jesus Christ. With over 1 million copies in print worldwide, and translated into more than a dozen languages, *Pigs in the Parlor* remains the authoritative book on the subject of deliverance.

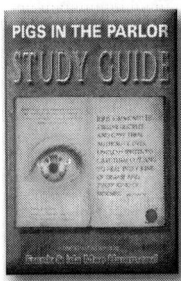

Study Guide: Pigs in the Parlor   0892281995

Designed as a study tool for either individuals or groups, this guide will enable you to diagnose your personal deliverance needs, walk you through the process of becoming free, and equip you to set others free from demonic torment. Includes questions and answers on a chapter-by-chapter basis as well as new information to further your knowledge of deliverance.

Overcoming Rejection   0892281057

Frank Hammond addresses the all-too-common root problem of rejection and the fear of rejection in the lives of believers, and provides steps to be set free. Learn how past experiences can influence our actions, and how we can be made whole.

The Breaking of Curses   089228109x

The Bible refers to curses more than 230 times, and 70 sins that cause curses are put forth in Scripture. Learn how Curses are just as real today as in Biblical times. This book shows what curses are and how you may deliver yourself and your family from them.

A Manual for Children's Deliverance 0892280786

The Hammonds' book for ministering to children is a valuable tool for parents to learn how to set their children free from spiritual bondages. Learn the basics of how to effectively minister deliverance to children.

9780892283682

THE DISCERNING OF SPIRITS

We are equipped by God for spiritual warfare through the gifts of the Holy Spirit mentioned in 1 Corinthians 12. God has said that these are the channels through which His power will flow, the avenues through which His Holy Spirit will operate. Chief among these gifts for the ministry of deliverance is the gift of the *discerning of spirits*. Frank Hammond explains the application of this gift to the believer, and provides examples of how it has worked in his own ministry.

9780892283859

PRAISE: A WEAPON OF WARFARE & DELIVERANCE

Praise is a powerful weapon in deliverance and spiritual warfare. As you praise the Lord, things begin to happen in the unseen realm. When Saul was troubled by an evil spirit, the only thing they knew to help him was to call David. When David began to play on his harp and sing praise to his God, the evil spirit departed from King Saul. A demon cannot exist in that atmosphere — he simply cannot function.

9780892283842

SPIRITUAL WARFARE FOR LOST LOVED ONES

Through spiritual warfare, intercessory prayer, and the ministry of love, we are able to help create the best possible environment around a loved one to come to know Jesus. But we must not lose our closeness with the Lord in the process, as these situations can be quite challenging to our spiritual walk. Frank Hammond says, "Don't let your family or friends go without resistance. Get in the spiritual battle, fight for your loves ones!"

9780892283903

POLTERGEISTS - DEMONS IN THE HOME

Do you, or someone you know, have demonic spirits in the home? Are you thrust out of sleep by banging doors, the sound of footsteps, lights going on and off? Do you see mysterious shadows on the wall or creatures at the foot of your bed? If so, there is good news for you. Your house can be cleansed! Just as the inside man can be swept clean of demonic spirits, so too can a house or a dwelling be swept clean from the evil presence and harassment of demonic spirits.

FRANK HAMMOND BOOKS & EBOOKS

CONFRONTING FAMILIAR SPIRITS   0892280174

A person can form and develop a close relationship with an evil spirit, willfully or through ignorance, for knowledge or gain. When a person forms a relationship with an evil spirit, he then has a familiar spirit. Familiar spirits are counterfeits of the Holy Spirit's work.

REPERCUSSIONS FROM SEXUAL SINS   0892282053

The sexual revolution has impacted our nation, our church and our family. Promiscuity, nudity and sexual obscenities have become commonplace. The inevitable consequence of defilement is the loss of fellowship with a holy God. Learn how to break free from the bondage of sexual sin.

THE MARRIAGE BED   0892281863

Can the marriage bed be defiled? Or, does anything and everything go so long as husband and wife are in agreement with their sexual activities? Drawing from God's emphasis on purity and holiness in our lives, this booklet explains how to avoid perverse sexual demonic activity in a home.

SOUL TIES   0892280166

Good soul ties covered include marriage, friendship, parent/child, between christians. Bad soul ties include those formed from fornication, evil companions, perverted family ties, with the dead, and demonic ties through the church. Learn how you can be set free from demonic soul ties.

OBSTACLES TO DELIVERANCE   0892282037

Why does deliverance sometimes fail? This is, in essence, the same question raised by Jesus' first disciples, when they were unable to cast out a spirit of epilepsy. Jesus gave a multi-part answer which leads us to take into account the strength of the spirit confronted and the strategy of warfare employed.

OBSTACLES TO DELIVERANCE   0892282037
Why does deliverance sometimes fail? This is, in essence, the same question raised by Jesus' first disciples, when they were unable to cast out a spirit of epilepsy. Jesus gave a multi-part answer which leads us to take into account the strength of the spirit confronted and the strategy of warfare employed.

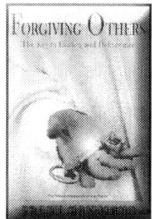
FORGIVING OTHERS   089228076X
Unforgiveness brings a curse, and can be a major roadblock to the deliverance and freedom of your soul. Find the spiritual truths regarding the necessity of forgiveness and the blessings of inner freedom which result!

THE SAINTS AT WAR   0892281049
Frank Hammond presents a study in warfare in the heavenlies, and explains how to pray for families, churches, cities and nations. Learn how each Christian is equipped as a soldier, and how Christians can change lives, families, communities and nations, and more!

THE FATHER'S BLESSING   0892280743
The body of Christ is missing out on something of great significance - The Father's Blessing. The Patriarchs of the Old Testament (Abraham, Isaac, Jacob) all practiced it. The effects of such a blessing are far reaching, and can readily make the difference between success & failure, victory & defeat, happiness & misery.

PROMOTED BY GOD   089228093X
How did Frank Hammond receive his powerful anointing to minister healing and deliverance for the Lord? Find out in his personal testimony, Promoted by God. Also, find answers to the questions: Is the Baptism in the Holy Spirit for today?, What was the purpose of this baptism? What were the qualifications for it? Were tongues a part of this experience? Did tongues have any useful purpose?

DVD VIDEOS

BY FRANK HAMMOND
DVD TEACHING SERIES

   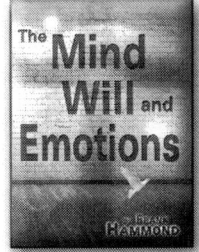

* All DVDs are U.S.A. NTSC Standard

AUDIO CDs

BY FRANK HAMMOND
AUDIO TEACHING SERIES

Watch & listen to excerpts now at:
www.impactchristianbooks.com/frank

The Audio Deliverance Series
(on Compact Disc)

Frank Hammond covers the basics of deliverance and includes an in-depth discussion of the groupings of demonic spirits. Also included is an explanation of the root spirits of Rejection and Rebellion, how to maintain deliverance, and how to distinguish between impulses of the flesh and impulses of demonic spirits.

There are 7 CDs included in this series, including the following titles:

- Healing the Personality
- The Schizophrenia Revelation, (I & II)
- Maintaining Deliverance
- Dealing with Pressures
- Demonic Doorways
- Group Ministry

Listen to an excerpt now at:
www.impactchristianbooks.com/deliverance

Website: WWW.IMPACTCHRISTIANBOOKS.COM

Phone Order Line: (314)-822-3309

Address: IMPACT CHRISTIAN BOOKS
332 LEFFINGWELL AVE. SUITE #101
KIRKWOOD, MO 63122

Made in the USA
San Bernardino, CA
29 March 2017